"Life is Difficult" and O.T.S.D

By: Joseph G. Lynch LCSW, CSOPT

Published by Joseph G. Lynch at Smashwords

TABLE OF CONTENTS

FORWARD

Dr. Scott Peck in his popular psychology book "The Road Less Traveled" has an opening line in the first chapter: "Life is difficult." I find that to be the case. Life is difficult without even doing anything to invite difficulties into our lives. This book is about my journey during a time that my life became much more difficult. The letters O.T.S.D. stand for "Ongoing Traumatic Stress Disorder" and is a new way of thinking about trauma. I found that P.T.S.D. - Post Traumatic Stress Disorder did not quite account for the nature of coping with ongoing exposure to trauma – trauma that is beyond the individual's control. With this book I am practicing a principle of 12 step groups: "I share my strength, hope and experience."

Chapter 1: How it all started

I was on vacation last week. I had cut the grass prior to the vacation and now it needed cutting again. But it was raining so the grass could not be cut that weekend. On Wednesday it was dry and the weather service was predicting rain again for Thursday so Wednesday night after work was the day to do the cutting. The yard is small - less than ¼ of an acre. Using the self-propelled walk behind mower I started on the front lawn and made about four passes back and forth - a total of maybe 50 yards. And then it started - the pain in my hips. The pain started out gradually at first and then began building. I kept going, walking a little slower and then eventually down to a hobble behind the mower. By the time I put the mower away about an hour later I was in lots of pain and my balance was off. I very gingerly walked back to the house.

This was not a crisis. The pain and hobbling was familiar to me. It was one outcome of a long journey that started on August 26, 2000. I had an active life. I loved to play golf but did not play it very well. I loved to be out on the course walking 18 holes, carrying my bag or maybe using my little pull cart up and down the hills. I would call my buddy Ron and we might get in 9 or 12 holes after work one evening. Then we would go to a local restaurant and have some dinner and have selective memory about our shots out on the course. I needed more selective memory than Ron. Ron was about 7 years older than I and our buddy Jim was about 20 years older than I. They were both better golfers than me. I also had a buddy David that played about like me but he was a busy attorney and had several children so he did not get out on the links with us quite so often. All of us enjoyed each other's company out on the course. All of us enjoyed walking. Jim had an electric cart with a remote control that would drive his bag down the fairway while he walked in the woods looking for brand new golf balls that someone had just put there the previous day.

At 48 I was not really athletic or in good shape but I could enjoy walking up and down the hills at my local golf course. But on August 26, 2000 I woke up with a sharp pain in my chest on my right side. I called my Doctor and was able to get into see him that morning. He did not like the looks of things and said I needed to go to the hospital. I said OK I will drive on over. He said no you don't understand, you need to go to the hospital and you are not driving yourself there - it is either the Rescue Squad or a friend but you are not driving. I called my buddy Ron but could not get him so I called my buddy David and he had time to get me to the hospital.

This part is a bit of a blur to me. My functioning began to go downhill fast. The pain in my chest kept increasing. I was getting various tests and was put on some pain medication and became a bit groggy. David stayed with me for a good part of that day. My family was in Baltimore, Maryland - about a 3.5 hour drive away so they could not help right this minute. I told David that my girlfriend of just about 3 months - Trish - was to meet me at my office at the end of the day and could he go over to the office and let her know what was going on with me. Trish told me later that as she arrived in the ER and came in to see me that my skin was ash colored and I was not very responsive. They put me on heart monitors and admitted me to the cardiac unit of the hospital. At some point in the middle of the night they brought in a portable X-Ray machine and did a chest X-Ray. My symptoms began to subside and I was able to stop the pain medication. At the end of a few days we had no explanation for the episode that led to my hospital admission and had no diagnosis but the chest X-Ray showed a spot on the left lung. The doctors wanted me to follow up with a pulmonary specialist.

I went to see the pulmonary specialist. He did a CT scan. I had never been a smoker so I was not too worried. The CT scan showed something high in my lung. The pulmonary specialist wanted to do a bronchoscopy procedure. This involved going over to the hospital and having some medication to numb up my throat, placing the scope through my nose and down my throat and then up into my lung. I was awake during all of this but a bit groggy. I could tell something was not going quite as planned. Apparently this growth in my lung was very high up in the lung and difficult to reach. There was some sort of minor malfunction with the scope and they tried to get a biopsy of the growth but could not reach it. My pulmonary specialist said that I needed further evaluation by a thoracic surgeon and he scheduled an appointment for me at the University of Virginia Medical Center (UVA) located a little over an hour away in Charlottesville, Virginia.

My girlfriend worked in Charlottesville as a Social Worker for a Hospice program so she was familiar with UVA and agreed to meet me over there the day of the appointment. We agreed to meet at the information desk. This was my first time at UVA. UVA is a large medical center teaching hospital. I parked my car in the multi-level parking deck and went in the door and saw an information desk and asked the receptionist where the Department of Thoracic Surgery was located. She said "We don't have a Department of Thoracic Surgery". I said sure you do I have an appointment with Dr. Thomas Daniel in that Department. She said Dr. Daniel is with the Cancer Center and gave me directions to the Cancer Center. That was the first time anyone had mentioned the "C" word to me. I was in shock. My girlfriend was nowhere to be seen so in a daze I went over to the Cancer Center. A few minutes later my girlfriend showed up. We discovered that UVA has multiple information desks. There is a big main desk at the front entrance - I missed that one completely and went into a little door and found a little information desk. So we had missed each other. But Trish had Dr. Daniel's name so she too discovered that the appointment was at the Cancer Center.

My mom had breast cancer. I had one of my social work field experiences at John's Hopkins Hospital Cancer Center. I had seen a lot of cancer patients and the often devastating impact on the patient and the family. My girlfriend worked in Hospice and had seen many cancer patients and their families through the stages of death and dying. She had worked with the families in their grief work. Both of us were in shock but also aware of the reality we had just stepped into. Cancer is a powerful word. It is a life changing diagnosis. We spent the day at UVA taking multiple test and procedures. At the end of the day we sat with Dr. Daniel and he said:

"You have a large bloody irregular mass high in your lung,
I am highly suspicious that it is cancer,
I think you should have it taken out."

We made the appointment for the surgery and we stayed in a daze for a good while after that day. The surgery was set for October. When the results of the biopsy showed it was not cancer we were shocked again but in a good way. The mass instead was formed from some scar tissue that may have formed when I had pneumonia one time. They took out the mass and also about a third of my left lung. I can't express the relief we felt with such good news. I don't know how many people go into the UVA cancer center being told that the Doctors think you have cancer but end up with no diagnosis of cancer. It has to be a small number. I was thanking God for the gift of life and no cancer.

My brother had brought my mom down from Baltimore to be with me during recovery. So after the surgery when I was in my room waking up my mom was there with me. Family and friends came in to visit. I felt overwhelmed physically and emotionally. The nurse came in and was about to do something - maybe change a dressing and I whispered to her "privacy" and she ushered out all of the visitors. When my mom came back in the room I was in tears and told her I could not handle that many people. I was surprised at how emotionally labile I was. I seemed to tear up with very little changes in my environment. Later I talked to my surgeon about it and he said: "Joe your body has just been through a trauma, you are going to be emotional." It made sense to me that trauma would cause emotional reactions. As a Clinical Social Worker I had worked with many clients who had Post Traumatic Stress Disorder. I just had not really identified myself as a "trauma survivor." Before I had the surgery I was talking with a physician friend and he cautioned me to remember that "surgery is just a planned stabbing" and his words echoed back to me as my trauma reactions occurred.

When I was in the hospital I went from ICU to the medical floor and I counted nine different tubes of some sort coming out of me. I had been on the medical floor for a few hours when Annie came into my room. Annie said "We are going to get you up and walking today, you can't spend all day in that bed." I looked at all the tubes and laughed and said "If you can figure out a way to walk with all this stuff coming out of me then we can go for a walk." Annie said "No problem." She came back in a few hours and said now is time for your walk. We took our time first just getting me to sit up in the bed without falling over, then my legs over the side of the bed, then standing next to the bed. Annie had a walker with wheels on it and many baskets. We put another hospital gown on me to cover my backside. There was a big suction machine that was pulling fluid from two chest tubes so we put that machine in one of the baskets. We grabbed an IV pole that had a pain medication pump and IV fluids. We hooked the catheter bag onto one of the rails of the walker. And we took whatever other tubes and devices that were hooked into me and put them on that cart. And then Annie and I went for a walk. Annie and I would take many walks over my years at UVA. By the time I was at UVA for my last lung surgery Annie had retired and I missed our walks together.

Chapter 2: Guillian-Barré Syndrome

After about a week in the hospital I was discharged. My recovery was going well. It was flu season so my doctor recommended that it would be a good idea to get a flu shot and a pneumonia vaccine to have better protection that winter. I had the shots then got a sinus infection. I never had one of those before. I was placed on an antibiotic and that seemed to clear things up. I had lunch at a Chinese restaurant that next week. I felt a little funny afterwards- sort of some numbness in my hands. I thought maybe they used too much MSG in the food and I was having a reaction. But things started getting worse. My hands were numb most of the time and my feet started to get numb too. I had some difficulty walking and some difficulty with balance. I went to my doctor and he gave me the Romberg Neurological Test. When I describe this test you may know it as the policeman's field sobriety test:

"Stretch out your arms to your side shoulder height, close your eyes and take the pointer finger of your right hand and touch your nose"

I failed. I fell over and into the doctor.

"Walk heel to toe across the floor."

I fell over. I was stunned and shocked. I thought
"What was going on with me?"

The doctor sent me to the Emergency Room (ER). I had a work up there, EKG, EMG, other test and clinical evaluation by the ER doctor. The doctor could find nothing wrong with me and he sent me home. I kept getting worse. It was the week before Christmas and I went with my daughter, Emily, to a tree lot and bought a Christmas tree. When we came home I could not lift my foot up the height of the curb going into my house. My daughter held onto me and I pulled myself up the steps by grabbing the railing and dragging my body up the 6 steps. I had a very difficult night. The next day I could not open a bottle of soda. I decided to go back to the ER. This time I was evaluated by a neurologist. I failed the Romberg Neurological Test - again - even worse failure than a few days previously. The neurologist said I needed to be admitted to a hospital but not my local hospital. I needed to go to UVA and if they did not have a bed in the neurological unit then I needed to go to the Medical College of Virginia in Richmond, Virginia - about 3 hours' drive away. This sounded familiar so I said OK I can get a friend to drive me over. He said no you don't understand, you need to go to UVA and no friend is driving you over you are going by ambulance. I really did not understand the gravity of the situation at that time. The neurologist suspected I had Guillian-Barré Syndrome (GBS). Almost everyone mispronounces it. Guillain-Barré (Ghee-yan Bah-ray) Syndrome is an inflammatory disorder of the peripheral nerves outside the brain and spinal cord. Dr. Guillain and Dr. Barré, two French physicians published their findings in 1916. It's also called: Acute Inflammatory Demyelinating Polyneuropathy and Landry's Ascending Paralysis. Below is a brief description:

Guillain-Barre syndrome is a rare disorder that causes your immune system to attack your peripheral nervous system (PNS). The PNS nerves connect your brain and spinal cord with the rest of your body. Damage to these nerves makes it hard for them to transmit signals. As a result, your muscles have trouble responding to your brain. No one knows what causes the syndrome. Sometimes it is triggered by an infection, surgery, or a vaccination.

The first symptom is usually weakness or a tingling feeling in your legs. The feeling can spread to your upper body. In severe cases, you become almost paralyzed. This is life-threatening. You might need a respirator to breathe. Symptoms usually worsen over a period of weeks and then stabilize.

Guillain-Barre can be hard to diagnose. Possible tests include nerve tests and a spinal tap. Most people recover. Recovery can take a few weeks to a few years. Treatment can help symptoms, and may include medicines or a procedure called plasma exchange.

NIH: National Institute of Neurological Disorders and Stroke
http://www.nlm.nih.gov/medlineplus/guillainbarresyndrome.html

So later I learned that the reason for the ambulance ride was concern that the GBS was advancing so fast that I could go into respiratory failure on the way to UVA. At UVA I underwent several treatments called plasmapheresis:

Plasmapheresis is a process involving the following steps:
−Whole blood is withdrawn from the person.

*–The liquid portion or plasma is removed from the blood
and replaced.*
*–The blood, with all its red and white blood cells, is
transfused back into the person.*
*This process is a successful method for treating some
autoimmune diseases such as myasthenia gravis and Guillain-Barré
syndrome, because it removes the circulating antibodies that are
thought to be active in these diseases.*

http://www.nationalmssociety.org/about-multiple-
sclerosis/what-we-know-about-
ms/treatments/medications/plasmapheresis-plasma-
exchange/index.aspx

I had lost the ability to walk, I could not make intelligible
speech, and at night I had to sleep with eye patches and cotton balls
covering my eyes as the nerve endings in my eyelids would not close
and my eyes could dry out and be damaged. The GBS skipped my
lungs and went to my head and face. I was extremely lucky to not
have my lungs involved in the GBS especially so soon after lung
surgery. I was a bit of an anomaly to the neurological residents at
UVA.

*"In the United States, for example, an estimated 3,000 to
6,000 people develop GBS each year on average, whether or not
they received a vaccination. This is about 1 to 2 cases of GBS per
100,000 people... In 1976, there was a small risk of GBS following
influenza (swine flu) vaccination (approximately 1 additional case
per 100,000 people who received the swine flu vaccine). That
number of GBS cases was slightly higher than the background rate
for GBS. Since then, numerous studies have been done to evaluate if
other flu vaccines were associated with GBS. In most studies, no
association was found, but two studies suggested that approximately
1 additional person out of 1 million vaccinated people may be at risk
for GBS associated with the seasonal influenza vaccine.*
http://www.cdc.gov/h1n1flu/vaccination/gbs_qa.htm

So the reality was that the chances of seeing an acute case of
GBS during neurological residency training were a bit rare. All of
the neurological residents came to visit me. They would remove the
top sheet from my bed and while I was lying there they would stick
safety pins in my legs. I could not feel anything but frequently when
they left my sheets were bloody. This would not be the last time that

I presented at UVA with some medical anomaly. Over the years I would get to know several medical specialists at UVA. For diagnosing GBS they did several tests on me - a spinal tap, nerve conductivity testing and some others. Some of these tests were difficult, painful, and seemed a bit more like a torturer technique then a medical procedure. Just my impression, someone else might describe it differently.

After a week I was discharged on Christmas Eve. I could walk slowly with a walker. I went to church that night for Christmas Eve service. It was crowded and I was glad I had the walker as it kept people away from my legs and feet which were not yet working all that well.

After I was out of the hospital about a week I returned to the UVA neurology clinic for a follow up appointment. My daughter, Emily, took me to the appointment. I was walking fairly well if I had the walker with me. I had never been to the UVA neurology clinic so I did not know how far it was from where we had parked the car to the clinic. It was a tremendously long way for someone in my condition. I managed to get to the appointment and that went fine. It was walking back that I experienced one of the most profound moments in my life. UVA has many long hallways that connect one building to another - many times the hallways are in the basement. As I was walking along one of those very long basement hallways I realized I could not make it. I did not have the strength and the stamina to walk any more down that hallway. I was immediately overwhelmed with a feeling of shame. I knew it did not make any rational sense - but the feeling of shame has nothing to do with rational thinking. I had been a fully functioning man just a few weeks previously and now I could not walk down a hallway. I burst into tears, I buried my head into the wall, and I did not want my daughter or anyone else to see what a pathetic person I was at that moment. An orderly came by and offered to get me a wheel chair. I could not say yes. I went deeper into shame and despair. I must have stayed in that hallway for over half an hour unable to move, unable to admit my limitations, unable to accept the drastic change in my body and my ability to function at the basic level of walking down a hallway. That experience has burned itself in my memory, in my soul and in the deepest and darkest places in my psyche. I have never fully shaken that feeling and even now as I write about it my eyes fill with tears and I want to hide. But it is important in telling my experience that I don't minimize or leave out that part of my experience- it may help someone else to know that this can happen.

Back at home I saw the neurologist who diagnosed me at the ER. He would frequently do that test where you hang your leg over the examining table and they hit your knee with that little rubber hammer. That is testing for nerve conductivity. If your leg bounces out then the electrical circuit made a complete loop. My leg did not move. It was about 6 months before that reflex returned. The GBS destroys the myelin sheathing around the nerves and it grows back at a very slow rate. I found out that balance is a complicated process. Your feet send electrical information to your brain so you can know where you are in space. I could not get the electrical information from my feed due to *neuropathy*.

Neuropathy: a result of nerve damage, often causes weakness, numbness and pain, usually in your hands and feet, but it may also occur in other areas of your body. People generally describe the pain of peripheral neuropathy as tingling or burning, while they may compare the loss of sensation to the feeling of wearing a thin stocking or glove

Also visual reference information is extremely important in order to have balance. I found this out the hard way several months after my hospitalization. I was at my in-laws home. It was night time and they live out in the country so it was pretty dark. I had forgotten something in my car. I stepped out of the kitchen and onto the back porch and was about to go down two steps into the driveway. There was a motion detector activated light that pointed toward the parking spaces in the driveway but you had to go about another foot before you were in the field to activate the light. Having closed the kitchen door behind me and opened the back porch door I lost all visual reference information in the dark. I could not move. I had no idea where my feet were without being able to visually see my feet - there was just not enough light. I could feel the back porch door with my hand so I hung onto that very tightly. I was frozen - could not go forward or backwards. I took my free hand and started waving - after a few tries I activated the motion detector light and was able to walk once again. My balance is still not so good. I have a few key rings that I carry - house keys, work keys, car keys - and each one has a little flashlight on it. I also purchased a flashlight application for my cell phone. I carry the cell phone on my belt at almost all times. When I turn out the light at night to go upstairs to bed, I first turn on my cell phone flashlight application so I can see my feet as I walk up the stairs. I try to avoid low light situations. I can still become frozen and not be able to move.

Chapter 3: Paecilomyces variotii

It took several months but I recovered. I could walk and even play golf again. Trish and I continued to date and in July 2002 we were married. We were celebrating our life together and enjoying my good health and recovery. We had a few very good health years. Then in 2005 I began to have difficulty again. I caught a cold. It seemed just like your routine cold. The kind as Ron says "If you have a cold it will last about a week to get over it - if you go to the doctor it will last about 7 days." But this cold kept lasting longer and longer. I went to the doctor and he diagnosed bronchitis and put me on an antibiotic. I took that for the required time and still no improvement. I had a chest X-Ray and there was a spot again in my left lung. With my history of a lung mass and a lung resection the doctor ordered a PET scan. Below is a description of a PET scan:

A positron emission tomography (PET) scan is an imaging test that uses a radioactive substance called a tracer to look for disease in the body. A PET scan shows how organs and tissues are working. This is different than magnetic resonance imaging (MRI) and computed tomography (CT), which show the structure of and blood flow to and from organs. A lung positron emission tomography (PET) scan is an imaging test that uses a radioactive substance (called a tracer) to look for disease in the lungs, particularly lung cancer. A PET scan requires a small amount of radioactive material (tracer). This tracer is given through a vein (IV), usually on the inside of your elbow. It travels through your blood and collects in organs and tissues. The tracer helps the

radiologist see certain areas or diseases more clearly. You will need to wait nearby as the tracer is absorbed by your body. This usually takes about 1 hour. Then, you will lie on a narrow table, which slides into a large tunnel-shaped scanner. The PET scanner detects signals from the tracer. A computer changes the results into 3-D pictures. The images are displayed on a monitor for your doctor to read. You must lie still during test. Too much movement can blur images and cause errors. The test takes about 90 minutes.
http://www.nlm.nih.gov/medlineplus/ency/article/007342.htm

I had a difficult time with the PET scan because I was in pain and staying still for 90 minutes was a challenge for me. When the test was done I had great difficulty with movement. They put me in a wheel chair and took me out to the waiting room to see Trish. Again this was one of those moments that I burst into tears and was an emotional mess just overwhelmed with the trauma. The results of the PET scan showed that the mass did uptake the dye and made it very suspicious for lung cancer.

So I went back to see Dr. Daniel at UVA. He ordered a needle biopsy to actually get a sample of the mass to make a conclusive diagnosis. The needle biopsy was a procedure where I had a CT scan and while undergoing the CT scan they placed a needle through my chest and into the mass in the lung to try and take a biopsy of the mass. I was awake but I was on a good bit of the narcotic Vicodin. As they maneuvered the needle into the mass I screamed out in pain. That was not supposed to happen with me being on the narcotic. They backed out the needle and the attending physician was called in and they tried again - again I screamed out in pain. (The reason for the pain would not become clear until much later during the surgery.) They took the needle out. They did have a biopsy but the procedure did not go as they expected. The biopsy turned out to be a type of fungus called Paecilomyces variotii

Paecilomyces is a fungal genus which can be found widely distributed around the world in dirt, food, and dead plant material. Many environments including homes naturally have some Paecilomyces species, and this fungus does not generally cause deleterious health effects, except in people with compromised immune systems. Paecilomyces variotii is a commonly occurring species in air and food, but it is also associated with many types of

human infections and is among the emerging causative agents of
opportunistic mycoses in immunocompromised hosts
<http://jcm.asm.org/content/48/8/2754.full and
http://www.wisegeek.com/what-is-paecilomyces.htm

This type of fungus is so common that it was assumed that the biopsy sample had become contaminated somewhere in the process and the test result was not felt to be valid. However my functioning was continuing to be compromised and Dr. Daniel recommended surgery to remove the mass and more of the lung. Again he was suspicious of cancer based on the PET scan results and the clinical presentation. We scheduled surgery. It was supposed to be about a 3 hour surgery. After 5 hours Dr. Daniel came out to the waiting room and spoke with Trish and Emily. When he opened me up he was expecting to find a soft tissue mass to remove from the lung. Instead he found a calcified fungal mass that had surrounded the aortic artery. He had to painstakingly chip the concrete like substance away without nicking the aortic artery. If he hit the aortic artery I could bleed out and die. He reported that he had been successful getting the mass out and not cutting the artery. However in the process he believed that he had cut some nerve endings and he believed my left lung would not re-inflate and he believed he had cut the nerves to my vocal chords and I would never speak again. We would not know for sure until I woke up. My experience with surgeons is that they don't come and tell you they believe they made an error without being really sure that they had made an error. Dr. Daniel had over 30 years' experience as a thoracic surgeon so I think he clearly believed the lung would not re-inflate and that I would never speak again. In my opinion two miracles happened that day - I woke up and the lung re-inflated and I was able to speak. One of my conclusions was "God is not done using my voice." Every day since I thank God for every word I get to speak and every day I get to be alive for one more day.

So it turns out the needle biopsy test was correct, I did have a Paecilomyces variotii fungal mass infection in my lung. To have that type of infection in a patient who was not immunocompromised was another medical anomaly. Usually a cancer patient or an AIDS patient might get this type of infection but it was very rare to see in a patient like me.

After my follow up appointments with Dr. Daniel he referred me to a pulmonary specialist to follow up with my lung and fungal situation. The pulmonary specialist did a CT scan and found new spots on the lung. We did not know what these were. We took periodic CT scans and the spots did not grow or change shape or size, they stayed small but did not go away. After several months the pulmonary specialist said to me: "Joe I am going to refer you to the Infectious Disease Division. You don't have an infectious disease but they specialize in weird stuff and you have weird stuff." Now I know "weird stuff" is not in the diagnosis book but I was glad for his honesty. One more time I knew that I was a medical anomaly.

I met the infectious disease doctor, Dr. Petri - yes really just like the petri dish from your biology class. He was a good doctor who really did know a lot about "weird stuff" like the fungus in my lung. He started me on an anti-fungal medication- Voriconazole.

Voriconazole is used to treat serious fungal infections such as invasive aspergillosis (a fungal infection that begins in the lungs and spreads through the bloodstream to other organs) Voriconazole is in a class of antifungal medications called triazoles. It works by slowing the growth of the fungi that cause infection.
http://www.nlm.nih.gov/medlineplus/druginfo/meds/a605022.html#special-dietary

Voriconazole is a very powerful drug. It does not mix well with many other drugs and your liver can get quite offended by this medication. I was on this drug for 6 months and the CT scans continued to show the spots on the lung but again with no changes in size or shape. We decided that if it was Paecilomyces variotii fungus that the 6 months of treatment killed it and it was safer to stop the medication at that time.

Chapter 4: AAA- No not the American Automobile Association

I had a reprieve from surgery, lung mass, fungus, doctors and medical stuff for a while. Things seemed to be relatively peaceful from 2005 to December of 2006. In December 2006 I was at a craft show at the fairgrounds and began to feel ill. I started to vomit violently and Trish got me home but I continued to have violent vomiting and dry heaves so we went to the hospital. In the ER I kept up the same thing only I aspirated some of the vomit into my lungs and caught pneumonia. I stayed in the hospital. Trish went home and then she and my son Ben began to get ill with the same virus and they were both bed-ridden. We had to have some friends come over and help out. I developed an Ileus in my bowel.

An Ileus is a partial or complete non-mechanical blockage of the small and/or large intestine. The term "ileus" comes from the Latin word for colic. There are two types of intestinal obstructions, mechanical and non-mechanical.

Non-mechanical obstruction, called ileus or paralytic ileus, occurs because peristalsis stops. Peristalsis is the rhythmic contraction that moves material through the bowel. Ileus is most often associated with an infection of the peritoneum (the membrane lining the abdomen). It is one of the major causes of bowel obstruction in infants and children. Another common cause of ileus is a disruption or reduction of the blood supply to the abdomen. Handling the bowel during abdominal surgery can also cause peristalsis to stop, so people who have had abdominal surgery are more likely to experience ileus. When ileus results from abdominal surgery the condition is often temporary and usually lasts only 48-72 hours. Overall, the total rate of bowel obstruction due both to mechanical and non-mechanical causes is one in one thousand people (1/1,000).
http://medical-dictionary.thefreedictionary.com/Ileus

Apparently not as rare as GBS but still it required scans of my abdomen to monitor the progress of the Ileus to see if it was clearing up on its own or if some other intervention was needed. The Ileus began to clear up in a day or two. However when they were taking scans of my abdomen they discovered an Abdominal Aortic Aneurysm.

Abdominal aortic aneurysm: A balloon-like swelling in the wall of the aorta within the abdomen. This swelling weakens the aorta's wall and, because of the great volume of blood flowing under high pressure in the aorta, it can rupture. An abdominal aortic aneurysm is monitored by ultrasound. Surgery is often recommended if the aneurysm is more than 5.5 centimeters (2.2 inches) in diameter or if a smaller aneurysm is enlarging with unusual rapidity.

I was discharged with a recommendation that I meet with a vascular surgeon at UVA. In January 2007 I met with Dr. Kenneth Cherry, Head of the Heart and Vascular Center at UVA. He ordered a more comprehensive CT scan and found two more aneurysms and they were all of the size that required surgery to avoid rupture. So we scheduled surgery for April 2007. When Dr. Cherry opened up my abdomen and was repairing the three aneurysms he discovered six more Abdominal Aortic Aneurysms. So all together there were 10 aneurysms:

1. Celiac artery aneurysm
2. Superior mesenteric artery aneurysm
3. Infrarenal abdominal aortic aneurysm
4. Abdominal aortic aneurysm
5 & 6. Bilateral common iliac artery aneurysms(2)
7 & 8. Bilateral hypogastric artery aneurysms(2)
9. Right external iliac artery aneurysms
10. Right renal artery aneurysm

The first surgery in April 2007 repaired the three aneurysms that they intended to repair. The other 7 would need to be scheduled for another surgery.

My brother Mike has a Masters of Library Science degree and is very knowledge about computers so I asked him to do a literature search on articles about patients with multiple aneurysms. He found an article where the patient had 4 aneurysms. Once again I got to be a medical anomaly. This never happens when I play the lottery only with medical conditions. I looked at an article on risk factors for aneurysms:

Risk Factors for aortic aneurysm and **Does Joe have that history**
History of smoking: NO
Family history of aortic aneurysm: NO
High blood pressure: YES
High cholesterol: NO
Atherosclerosis: NO
Inherited conditions such as Marfan's syndrome: NO

Below is a description of AAA:

Abdominal Aortic Aneurysms (AAA)In addition to the risk factors noted above, infection and trauma can also cause AAA, although most are associated with atherosclerosis.(3) A normal abdominal aorta is approximately 2.0 cm in diameter. An abdominal aneurysm places stress on the wall of the aorta. The risk of rupture for an AAA over 5cm in diameter is approximately 20%, over 6cm approximately 40%, and over 7cm over 50%. Rupture of an AAA carries a risk of death up to 90% (4). AAA is more common in men and in individuals aged 65 years and older. AAA is less common in women and with black race/ethnicity (5). AAA (from 2.9–4.9cm diameter) are present in 1.3% of men aged 45–54 years and 12.5% of men aged 75–84 years. Equivalent figures for women are 0% and 5.2% in each age group, respectively.6
http://www.cdc.gov/dhdsp/data_statistics/fact_sheets/fs_aortic_aneur ysm.htm

For me the surgery for repairing the AAA's involved an incision from just below my sternum to just below my belly button. Below is a description of the procedure:

Abdominal aortic aneurysm open repair. Open repair of an abdominal aortic aneurysm involves an incision of the abdomen to directly visualize the aortic aneurysm. The procedure is performed in an operating room under general anesthesia. The surgeon will make an incision in the abdomen either lengthwise from below the breastbone to just below the navel or across the abdomen and down the center. Once the abdomen is opened, the aneurysm will be repaired by the use of a long cylinder-like tube called a graft. Grafts are made of various materials, such as Dacron (textile polyester synthetic graft) or polytetrafluoroethylene (PTFE, a nontextile synthetic graft). The graft is sutured to the aorta connecting one end of the aorta at the site of the aneurysm to the other end of the aorta. Open repair remains the standard procedure for an abdominal aortic aneurysm repair.
http://www.hopkinsmedicine.org/healthlibrary/test_procedures/cardi ovascular/abdominal_aortic_aneurysm_repair_92,P08291/

AAA Prevalence

Approximately one in every 250 people over the age of 50 will die of a ruptured AAA. AAA affects as many as eight percent of people over the age of 65. Males are four times more likely to have AAA than females. AAA is the 17th leading cause of death in the United States, accounting for more than 15,000 deaths each year.

Those at highest risk are males over the age of 60 who have ever smoked and/or who have a history of atherosclerosis ("hardening of the arteries"). 50 percent of patients with AAA who do not undergo treatment die of a rupture
http://www.sirweb.org/patients/abdominal-aortic-aneurysms/

The initial surgery was successful. The aneurysms were repaired. However I had difficulty with eating, drinking and had constant diarrhea. I was discharged and continued to have difficulty with these items at home. I was becoming dehydrated. I returned for the second surgery in June and the other 7 aneurysms were repaired. However I again was having difficulty with eating, drinking and the constant diarrhea. I ended up back in the hospital. Some days I would go and spend all day at the hospital in a treatment room receiving IV fluids to keep me from being dehydrated. There were multiple times in treatment rooms or admitted to the hospital. I kept losing weight. I was a big man-6 feet tall and 270 pounds. I lost 20 pounds - then it was 50 pounds - then 100 pounds at 90 days post surgery. My wife worked in hospice, she knew I was wasting away and was dying. She estimated that if this process was not reversed I would be dead in the next few weeks. When I was awake I would try to consume fluids and after a day of trying I had consumed 3 ounces. I lost mental functioning. I could not concentrate. I could only attend to things about 1 to 2 feet from me, I did not have the physical or psychological energy to focus or attend to anything else. I was at peace. I was not anxious. I was just slowly disappearing and slowly disengaging from life.

Chapter 5: Coming back from the edge

At one of my hospitalizations Trish stepped in and told the doctor she was not taking me home and she insisted that I be evaluated by a gastroenterologist and a dietician. The dietician took one look at me and said I was starving to death and she put me on a nasogastric feeding tube treatment.

A nasogastric tube is used for feeding and administering drugs and other oral agents such as activated charcoal. For drugs and for minimal quantities of liquid, a syringe is used for injection into the tube. For continuous feeding, a gravity based system is employed, with the solution placed higher than the patient's stomach. If accrued supervision is required for the feeding, the tube is often connected to an electronic pump which can control and measure the patient's intake and signal any interruption in the feeding.

http://en.wikipedia.org/wiki/Nasogastric_intubation

My set up was for a gravity based system with the bag of liquid set on an IV pole and it went into my stomach for 9 hours at night while I was asleep. I did this for about 5 weeks. I began to be able to stay hydrated. Gradually I was able to add clear liquids. I graduated to Slim Fast after the feeding tube was no longer needed. As I progressed to more solid food I would occasionally have all of the symptoms return, nausea, vomiting, and diarrhea. When this would happen I would switch back to Slim Fast. It did not make sense but switching back to Slim Fast would correct the symptoms.

On death and dying

It was a bit of an odd experience being so close to death. A few years later a friend who had visited me in the hospital said "Joe if anyone told you that you looked good back then, they were lying." I did get to see many of my friends during that time. I went to church. There were two other men at church at that time that were wasting away as I was. Later people told me they wondered who would die first. One of them did die. I and the other fella recovered. But the process of seeing friends who take one look at you and know you are dying is a bit disconcerting. The friends know this is the last time they might see you alive and they go ahead and say their goodbyes to you then. It is sort of like being at your own wake. People tell you what they appreciated about you, they reminisce about old times and good times, and they are trying to manage their own emotions while at the same time they are trying not to upset you. For me I did not just get to say goodbye to one person, I got to say goodbye to everyone I knew. It was a strange mixture of honoring, humbling, depressing, and emotionally painful. I think that in facing death and then recovering something in me "snapped." I don't know exactly how to explain it but I had learned in a manner that can be learned in no other way what it meant to be alive and what it meant to be dying. I think it was Mark Twain who said "A man learns something by carrying a cat by the tail that he can learn in no other way." I was sort of like that man.

Clinical social worker

I am a clinical social worker. I provide individual, couples and family counseling. I have also been very active in my professional associations. In social work we talk about interventions at the "micro" and "macro" level. "Micro" deals with individuals, couples, families and small groups. "Macro" is more of a social policy, systems, politics, rules and regulations type of intervention to help groups of people not just the individual. So with my professional associations I had been active at the Macro level. In 2007 after I had stabilized a bit the National Association of Social Workers - Virginia Chapter awarded me their Lifetime Achievement Award. Below is an excerpt from my acceptance speech:

One of my first thoughts that came to mind when I was informed about being selected for lifetime achievement award was Wait a minute, I am not done yet! But they assured me that receiving the award would not stop NASW from tapping me to be on committees and advocating for social work.

I can't tell you the number of times I have called the chapter office over the years with an idea for a bill on some social work matter, only to find out that I just volunteered for a committee assignment. One of those times was back in the day before we had privileged communication for social work in Virginia. I called NASW VA to gather support and- you guessed it- I found out I just volunteered for the legislative committee. This effort was successful and today social work has privileged communication Code of Virginia 8.01-400.2.

After I learned that I was to receive the award I began to ponder "what are the characteristics that have led me to keep pushing for improvements in the social work profession over all of these years". Two characteristics stand out for me: Persistence and Spirituality. An example of persistence is that I began to develop an instrument -a questionnaire- that would ask behaviorally based questions about a social workers practice that might identify those social workers who might be on the "slippery slope" headed toward a boundary violation. I have been working on this for the last 20 years. When I have time I pull this project out and work on it, put it away for a while and then pull it back out again and again to try to tweak and focus this tool. I now provide it to practitioners at each ethics workshop I present.

In conclusion I want to mention the other important characteristic that has shaped my commitment over the years. That is the spiritual side of my process. All of us have experiences that sharpen our spiritual growth. For me one was September a year ago I was in UVA hospital, undergoing surgery from a UVA Cancer Center thoracic surgeon to remove a large mass and most of my left lung. I believe some miracles happened that day. After 5 hours the surgeon came out to my wife and daughter and reported that he had removed the calcified part of the mass from around my aortic artery but in the process he believed he had severed the nerve endings to my lung and that the lung would not re - inflate. Also he had severed the nerve ending to my vocal chords and I would never speak again.

My lung re inflated and as you can tell I am able to speak, to me, two miracles. I believe God is not done with using my voice to continue to advocate for our social work profession.

I am a member of another professional association, the Virginia Society for Clinical Social Work. In 2011 I was awarded

The Lifetime Achievement Award by the Virginia Society for Clinical Social Work. Below are excerpts from that presentation:

Joseph George Lynch, L.C.S.W., is a man for all seasons...and for many reasons. He is an ultimate man of conscience, remaining true to his principles under all circumstances at all times. He is a clinical social worker par excellence and a model man: devoted son, brother, husband, father, grandfather, clinician, churchman, entrepreneur, teacher, consultant, author, civic leader, social and political pioneer, volunteer, community activist, minority spokesman, public servant and defender of human rights.

Joseph George Lynch, L.C.S.W. is the first person granted The Lifetime Achievement Award by the Virginia Society for Clinical Social Work. Hereafter, The Award shall be known as THE JOSEPH GEORGE LYNCH, LC.S.W. LIFETIME ACHIEVEMENT AWARD and shall be granted from time to time by The Virginia Society for Clinical Social Work to persons recognized by The Society as having made outstanding contributions to human welfare, service to others and advancement of the field of clinical social work. Adopted by the Virginia Society for Clinical Work and affirmed this day, March 26, 2011

Dying changes your perspective on life

I did not end up dead, yet. But I did experience a good bit of the dying process. Very slowly I began to disengage from life. This was not a conscious decision it was more of a natural process of less and less physical, mental and psychic energy being available. I was aware that everything took energy out of me. To try to sip 6 ounces of liquid in a day was a major goal and I often failed. To listen to someone talk took mental and physical energy. I started sleeping more and more. I found eventually that I could only attend to things that were about two feet away from me- like an invisible force field. I could no longer focus on reading, watching TV, eating, drinking, even talking was an effort. I felt at peace, I was not distraught - that would have taken too much energy. I was just gradually disappearing - physically, mentally and emotionally. In some unconscious way I was preparing to let go of life. It was a bit of a surprise to me that I did not die after being so close to that psychological place of mostly disappearing from life.

Coming back to life after the experience of being in the dying process and close to death changed me in some deep ways. One change that occurred in me was that I stopped counting on there being a future for me. I did not want to schedule events more than a few weeks out. I knew that I just might not be around when that date arrived. I did not assume that I had a tomorrow. I became unable to invest emotion in future events. I had a difficult time investing emotion in my relationships. I knew that any day I could wake up and hear:

"You have a life threatening medical event going on and all of your plans for the rest of your life are on hold"

Or words to that effect. I did not do any of this changing with any conscious intent. It was more of a discovery. The conscious part was I developed a new motto:

"If I am not in the hospital today and I feel well and I want to do something, I am going to do it now"

This had several impacts. For one it kept me busy. I more frequently was using the OHIO rule - *"Only Handle It Once."* I took on projects that I thought I could do now not later. I think I developed a symptom that is called "psychic numbing."

Psychic numbing is a form of desensitization; it refers to incapacity to feel or to confront certain kinds of experience due to the blocking or absence of inner forms or imagery that can connect with such experiences (Litton, 1976, p.24).

Thus psychic numbing is not an "all of none" phenomenon which switches "on" and "off" like a light. Extending Lifton's definition, we find psychic numbing to be multidimensional and pertaining to:
 Emotions
 Psychoformative cognitive processes
 Capacity for self-monitoring
 Capacity to experience affects

Cessation in empathic attunement and
Loss of capacity for genuine interpersonal relations
Empathy in the Treatment of Trauma and PTSD,
By Rhiannon Thomas, John P. Wilson

I did not want to feel negative emotions. I did not want to feel fear, hopelessness, confusion, helplessness and depression. By unconsciously blocking the negative emotions I ended up blocking most emotions - negative and positive. I became "hypervigilant" about my body and my health.

Hypervigilance is an enhanced state of sensory sensitivity accompanied by an exaggerated intensity of behaviors whose purpose is to detect threats. Hypervigilance is also accompanied by a state of increased anxiety which can cause exhaustion. Other symptoms include: abnormally increased arousal, a high responsiveness to stimuli, and a constant scanning of the environment for threats.
http://en.wikipedia.org/wiki/Hypervigilance

I became like a fire fighter, always ready to drop everything and go fight a fire. Only my body was the building that was burning down. And my ability to actually fight the fire was pretty close to nothing.

There was nothing I could do to:
    -prevent another aneurysm for occurring.
    -prevent an aneurysm from rupturing.
    -prevent a lung mass from forming
    -prevent Paecilomyces variotii from forming.
    -prevent Guillain-Barré syndrome from occurring.
    -prevent the loss of 100 pounds in 90 days or to
    -prevent the need for a nasogastric tube.

Each time I was in a medical crisis I kept remembering a line from the movie "Hunt for Red October." Sean Connery plays the part of a Russian submarine Captain and at one point he is speaking to his crew and says:

"...Once again we play our dangerous game with the Americans..."

I would imagine that scene and think to myself:

"Once again we play our dangerous game with surgery"

Chapter 6: It's a long road back and I am not sure you can get there from here

All together I was out of work for 10 months and on short term disability. I decided to go back to work part-time and see if I could manage the strain and stress. I found that I tired easily and did not have much stamina. I was talking to a couple in my office doing marital therapy and I fell asleep in the middle of one of my sentences. I apologized profusely. I also went to see my sleep doctor. I had been diagnosed with sleep apnea twenty years ago. He did a sleep study all night and then the next day he continued the study by having me take a 20 minute nap every two hours while hooked up to all sorts of wires measuring many things.

There two main types of sleep, or ways of sleeping. The first is Rapid Eye Movement (REM) and the other is non-REM. It's during REM sleep that we dream, although only about 25% of our time sleeping is spent in this state. We spend the majority of the night sleeping in the non-REM stat.

After 70-90 minutes, you enter REM sleep.

Your eyes will flicker and dart rapidly in different directions during this time, while your breathing becomes more rapid, shallow and irregular. You have between three and five episodes of REM sleep each night—after each one ends, the sleep cycle repeats itself until you finally wake up in the morning. http://sleepinsider.com/2-rem-sleep.php

Well my sleep test results showed that each time I took a nap that I was in REM sleep in less than two minutes. This met the criteria for Narcolepsy which is described below:

Narcolepsy is a disorder marked by excessive daytime sleepiness, uncontrollable sleep attacks, and cataplexy (a sudden loss of muscle tone, usually lasting up to half an hour). Narcolepsy is the second-leading cause of excessive daytime sleepiness (after

obstructive sleep apnea). Persistent sleepiness and sleep attacks are the hallmarks of this condition. The sleepiness has been compared to the feeling of trying to stay awake after not sleeping for two or three days.

People with narcolepsy fall asleep suddenly—anywhere, at any time, maybe even in the middle of a conversation. These sleep attacks can last from a few seconds to more than an hour. Depending on where they occur, they may be mildly inconvenient or even dangerous to the individual. Some people continue to function outwardly during the sleep episodes, such as talking or putting things away. But when they wake up, they have no memory of the event.

Narcolepsy is related to the deep, dreaming part of sleep known as rapid eye movement (REM) sleep. Normally when people fall asleep, they experience 90 minutes of non-REM sleep, which is then followed by REM sleep. People with narcolepsy, however, enter REM sleep immediately. In addition, REM sleep occurs inappropriately throughout the day. There has been debate over the incidence of narcolepsy. It is thought to affect between one in every 1,000 to 2,000 Americans. The known prevalence in other countries varies, from one in 600 in Japan to one in 500,000 in Israel. Reasons for these differences are not clear.

Causes and symptoms

In 1999 researchers identified the gene that causes narcolepsy. The gene allows cells in the hypothalamus (the part of the brain that regulates sleep behavior) to receive messages from other cells. When this gene is abnormal, cells cannot communicate properly, and abnormal sleeping patterns develop.

The disorder sometimes runs in families, but most people with narcolepsy have no relatives with the disorder. Researchers believe that the inheritance of narcolepsy is similar to that of heart disease. In heart disease, several genes play a role in being susceptible to the disorder, but it usually does not develop without an environmental trigger of some sort.

While the symptoms of narcolepsy usually appear during the teens or 20s, the disease may not be diagnosed for many years. Most often, the first symptom is an overwhelming feeling of fatigue

Other symptoms of narcolepsy include:

1. Sleep attacks: short, uncontrollable sleep episodes throughout the day.
2. Sleep paralysis: a frightening inability to move shortly after awakening or dozing off.
3. Auditory or visual hallucinations: intense, sometimes terrifying experiences at the beginning or end of a sleep period
                http://medical-dictionary.thefreedictionary.com/narcolepsy
My sleep doctor prescribed some medication and I was able to keep awake during the day and sleep OK at night. I usually awake early in the morning about 4:00 AM. That is when I find myself writing things like this paper. I found that sometimes even on the medication that I would experience "break through narcolepsy" during the day and had to be prescribed a PRN (as needed) medication to take when that happened.

Just When You Think "It Is Safe to Go Back into the Water"

I continued to be followed by the vascular surgeon at UVA. One time I went for my appointment, had a CT scan and he said everything looked good. I called Trish and we decided to meet for dinner after work. Just prior to Trish arriving at my office so we could walk downtown to dinner I received a call on my cell phone from the vascular surgeon. He said the radiologist looked at my CT scan and everything was not fine. I had a problem with one of my aneurysms and needed surgery very soon. I thought of the expression *"Just when you think it is safe to go back in the water"* it all changes again.

In December 2009 I needed another AAA surgery in an attempt to repair 3 aneurysms that had become enlarged. This was not successful due to excessive bleeding and excessive scar tissue that had formed in the abdomen. The vascular surgeon backed out of the operation. He said in his 30 years of surgery he had backed out like that only 3 times. He also said he could not open me up like that again. He talked to Trish and asked if she understood what he was saying? She said "Yes." We all know it means if I get another AAA he can't operate, and if they can't use interventional radiology then eventually it will rupture and kill me. He had told me on a previous visit that "people who have aneurysms tend to get aneurysms" so it is likely I will have more of them.

In January 2010 an angioplasty procedure was completed that installed three stents in the abdominal arteries.

Definition: Angioplasty is the technique of mechanically widening a narrowed or obstructed blood vessel, typically as a result of atherosclerosis. An empty and collapsed balloon on a guide wire, known as a balloon catheter, is passed into the narrowed locations and then inflated to a fixed size using water pressures some 75 to 500 times normal blood pressure (6 to 20 atmospheres) https://www.medify.com/treatments-conditions/angioplasty-treatment-aortic-aneurysm

Interventional Repair - This minimally invasive technique is performed by an interventional radiologist using imaging to guide the catheter and graft inside the patient's artery. For the procedure, an incision is made in the skin at the groin through which a catheter is passed into the femoral artery and directed to the aortic aneurysm. Through the catheter, the physician passes a stent graft that is compressed into a small diameter within the catheter. The stent graft is advanced to the aneurysm, then opened, creating new walls in the blood vessel through which blood flows.

This is a less invasive method of placing a graft within the aneurysm to redirect blood flow and stop direct pressure from being exerted on the weak aortic wall. This relatively new method eliminates the need for a large abdominal incision. It also eliminates the need to clamp the aorta during the procedure. Clamping the aorta creates significant stress on the heart, and people with severe heart disease may not be able to tolerate this major surgery. Stent grafts are most commonly considered for patients at increased surgical risk due to age or other medical conditions. http://www.sirweb.org/patients/abdominal-aortic-aneurysms/

In August 2010 a CT scan of pelvis found the graft repairs to the iliac arteries had become twisted or "tortuous" and was restricting blood flow and causing pain in the hips and legs. An angioplasty procedure was performed in October 2010 to open up the restricted area and place stents in those areas.

The angioplasty procedures were successful in placing the stents in the aortic arteries however the restricted blood flow causing pain in the hips and legs improved only slightly and over time has become much worse. To look at me you think I look fine. But if I try to walk about 25 yards my hips and legs become painful. If I push it then my hands go numb and I am hobbling when I attempt to walk. Most of the time I try not to put myself in a situation where I have to walk more than 25 yards. When I can't avoid walking that far I have lots of pain, take lots of breaks, and if there is a place to sit down I sit down. I am worn out afterwards.

In August 2010 I experienced severe back and chest pain and was admitted to the local hospital overnight. They ruled out heart attack and discharge diagnosis was atypical chest pain-non cardiac.

In December 2011 when I got up in the morning and was trying to walk to the bathroom I began to fall into the wall. This worsened throughout the day and I ended up in the local hospital. They gave me the Romberg Neurological Test - I failed. I had given my medical history to the nurse. I hate to do this to someone nowadays because it is just such a litany of odd medical events. The ER doctor came in and after I failed the test we talked a bit. He said that when the nurse told him the medical history he said "Is this all the same patient?" He wanted to do an MRI. So I was sent down to the MRI lab but the guy there took one look at my history and said he was not going to touch me. He said that if a piece of metal had been placed in me during one of the surgeries then the MRI would cause it to rupture the aortic artery and I would bleed to death and he could not take that chance. I found out that the computer system at my local hospital and the computer system at UVA could not talk to each other to find out if there was any metal in me from the UVA procedures. So the ER doctor got on the phone with the UVA ER doctor and they worked out for me to be transported by ambulance to UVA.

At the UVA ER I fail the Romberg test again. The nurse begins to administer a mental status exam.

A mental status examination (MSE) is an assessment of a patient's level of cognitive (knowledge-related) ability, appearance, emotional mood, and speech and thought patterns at the time of evaluation. It is one part of a full neurologic (nervous system) examination and includes the examiner's observations about the patient's attitude and cooperativeness as well as the patient's answers to specific questions. The most commonly used test of cognitive functioning per se is the so-called Folstein Mini-Mental Status Examination (MMSE), developed in 1975. http://medical-dictionary.thefreedictionary.com/mental+status+examination

Now I am familiar with the mental status exam in my work as a Clinical Social Worker. But being familiar with the exam did not help any that day. The nurse started to ask me "What day of the week is it?", "What is the name of the hospital?"- I was doing OK so far. Then she asked me a typical mental status exam question "Who is the President of the United States?" Now the correct answer was Barack Obama. But I had no idea what the answer was. I thought maybe it was George Bush. But something told me that was not correct. Knowing it was not the correct answer did not help me at all to know the correct answer. I just stared at the nurse for about 45 seconds - it seemed like a lot longer. And finally Barack Obama came to me from somewhere very far back in my brain. I knew something was not right. I wondered if I had a cerebral aneurysm.

I had an MRI of my brain that night (no metal that would prohibit an MRI had been placed in me in any of the procedures). I did not have a cerebral aneurysm or a stroke. Over the next year I had several evaluations, including a nerve conductivity test, an inner ear evaluation, an evaluation to see if there were pinched nerves - all to rule out likely problems. All of the major things were ruled out. I contacted the neurologist and told him that when I take my car to my mechanic with an intermittent problem he tells me "Joe bring it back when it does it all the time and I can fix it." So I told the neurologist that when I was falling into walls all the time that I would be back. So far it is still intermittent.

Chapter 7: What is O.T.S.D.?

For many people in many parts of the world the following phrase is true each day:

"Bad things might happen at any moment and nothing you do will predict where or when and you don't have the power to prevent it from happening"

The diagnosis PTSD Post Traumatic Stress Disorder is now well known due to the many traumatic events that have occurred in recent years- 9/11, Operation Iraqi Freedom, Operation Enduring Freedom in Afghanistan, Genocide in the Democratic Republic of the Congo and the Boston Marathon bombing to mention a few traumatic events. One of the key elements to PTSD is the "P." The "P" stands for "Post." Inherent in that "Post" word is the fact that the traumatic event is over, it is in the past, or we are "Post" the traumatic event. But what if the traumatic event is not "Post" but is "ongoing". The member of the armed forces in Afghanistan each day is in an ongoing traumatic event situation. My medical journey is ongoing and has been ongoing since 2000. It is never "Post" for me as I am acutely aware that at any moment any day my world can all change in a heartbeat and I will be in a medical traumatic event again. There is never a time I psychologically "let my guard down."

Surprisingly the Diagnostic and Statistical Manual IV (DSM IV) - the book of psychiatric diagnoses published by the American Psychiatric Association, does not have a diagnosis of "Ongoing Traumatic Stress Disorder." So I am offering a description of "Ongoing Traumatic Stress Disorder - OTSG" with a comparison to Post Traumatic Stress Disorder-PTSD. It is very similar to "Post Traumatic Stress Disorder" but without the time frame of "Post." Below are listed each Criterion for PTSD followed by suggested Criterion for OTSD

POST TRAUMATIC STRESS DISORDER

Criterion A: stressor
The person was exposed to: death, threatened death, actual or threatened serious injury, or actual or threatened sexual violence, as follows: (1 required)
1. Direct exposure
2. Witnessing, in person.
3. Indirectly, by learning that a close relative or close friend was exposed to trauma. If the event involved actual or threatened death, it must have been violent or accidental
4. Repeated or extreme indirect exposure to aversive details of the event(s), usually in the course of professional duties (e.g., first responders, collecting body parts; professionals repeatedly exposed

to details of child abuse). This does not include indirect non-professional exposure through electronic media, television, movies, or pictures

OGOING TRAUMATIC STRESS DISORDER

Criterion A: stressor
The person was exposed to: death, an illness that threatens death, actual or threatened serious injury, or actual or threatened sexual violence, as follows: (1 required)
1. Direct exposure
2. Witnessing, in person
3. Indirectly, by learning that a close relative or close friend was exposed to trauma. The event involved actual or threatened death or a life threatening illness
4. Repeated or extreme indirect exposure to aversive details of the event(s), as in being a family member of a person who is dying

POST TRAUMATIC STRESS DISORDER

Criterion B: intrusion symptoms
The traumatic event is persistently re-experienced in the following way(s): (1 required)
1. Recurrent, involuntary, and intrusive memories. Note: Children older than 6 may express this symptom in repetitive play
2. Traumatic nightmares. Note: Children may have frightening dreams without content related to the trauma(s)
3. Dissociative reactions (e.g., flashbacks) which may occur on a continuum from brief episodes to complete loss of consciousness. Note: Children may reenact the event in play
4. Intense or prolonged distress after exposure to traumatic reminders
5. Marked physiologic reactivity after exposure to trauma-related stimuli.

OGOING TRAUMATIC STRESS DISORDER

Criterion B: intrusion symptoms
The traumatic event is persistently experienced in the following way(s): (1 required)
1. Recurrent, involuntary, and intrusive memories.
2. Traumatic nightmares.
3. Dissociative reactions (e.g., flashbacks) which may occur on a continuum from brief episodes to complete loss of consciousness.
4. Intense or prolonged distress with ongoing exposure to traumatic events.
5. Marked physiologic reactivity to ongoing trauma-related stimuli.

POST TRAUMATIC STRESS DISORDER

Criterion C: avoidance
Persistent effortful avoidance of distressing trauma-related stimuli after the event: (1 required)
1. Trauma-related thoughts or feelings.
2. Trauma-related external reminders (e.g., people, places, conversations, activities, objects, or situations).

OGOING TRAUMATIC STRESS DISORDER

Criterion C: avoidance
Persistent effortful avoidance of distressing trauma-related stimuli (1 required)
1. Trauma-related thoughts or feelings.
2. Trauma-related external reminders (e.g., people, places, conversations, activities, objects, or situations).

POST TRAUMATIC STRESS DISORDER

Criterion D: negative alterations in cognitions and mood
Negative alterations in cognitions and mood that began or worsened after the traumatic event: (2 required)
1. Inability to recall key features of the traumatic event (usually dissociative amnesia; not due to head injury, alcohol or drugs).

2. Persistent (and often distorted) negative beliefs and expectations about oneself or the world (e.g., "I am bad," "The world is completely dangerous.").
3. Persistent distorted blame of self or others for causing the traumatic event or for resulting consequences.
4. Persistent negative trauma-related emotions (e.g., fear horror, anger, guilt or shame).
5. Markedly diminished interest in (pre-traumatic) significant activities.
6. Feeling alienated from others (e.g., detachment or estrangement).
7. Constricted affect: persistent inability to experience positive emotions.

OGOING TRAUMATIC STRESS DISORDER

Criterion D: negative alterations in cognitions and mood
Negative alterations in cognitions and mood that are ongoing concurrently with traumatic events: (2 required).
1. Inability to recall key features of the one or more of the traumatic events (not due to head injury, alcohol or drugs).
2. Persistent (and often distorted) negative beliefs and expectations about oneself or the world.
(Belief that you are in control of traumatic events).
3. Persistent distorted blame of self or others for causing the traumatic event or for resulting consequences.
4. Persistent negative trauma-related emotions (e.g., fear, horror, anger, guilt or shame).
5. Markedly diminished interest in (pre-traumatic) significant activities.
6. Feeling alienated from others (e.g., detachment or estrangement).
7. Constricted affect: persistent inability to experience positive emotions.

POST TRAUMATIC STRESS DISORDER

Criterion E: alterations in arousal and reactivity
Trauma related alterations in arousal and reactivity that began or worsened after the traumatic event: (2 required)
1. Irritable or aggressive behavior.
2. Self-destructive or reckless behavior.
3. Hypervigilance.
4. Exaggerated startle response.
5. Problems in concentration.
6. Sleep disturbance.

OGOING TRAUMATIC STRESS DISORDER

Criterion E: alterations in arousal and reactivity
Trauma-related alterations in arousal and reactivity that are ongoing concurrently with the traumatic events: (2 required)
1. **Irritable or aggressive behavior.**
2. **Self-destructive or reckless behavior.**
3. **Hypervigilance.**
4. **Exaggerated startle response.**
5. **Problems in concentration.**
6. **Sleep disturbance.**

POST TRAUMATIC STRESS DISORDER

Criterion F: duration
Persistence of symptoms (in Criteria B, C, D and E) for more than one month.

OGOING TRAUMATIC STRESS DISORDER

Criterion F: duration
Ongoing symptoms (in Criteria B, C, D and E)

POST TRAUMATIC STRESS DISORDER

Criterion G: functional significance
Significant symptom-related distress or functional impairment (e.g., social, occupational).

OGOING TRAUMATIC STRESS DISORDER

Criterion G: functional significance
Significant symptom-related distress or functional impairment
(e.g., social, occupational)

POST TRAUMATIC STRESS DISORDER

Criterion H: attribution
Disturbance is not due to medication, substance use, or other illness.
Specify if: With dissociative symptoms.
In addition to meeting criteria for diagnosis, an individual
experiences high levels of either of the following in reaction to
trauma-related stimuli:
1. Depersonalization: experience of being an outside observer of or
detached from oneself (e.g., feeling as if "this is not happening to
me" or one were in a dream).
2. Derealization: experience of unreality, distance, or distortion
(e.g., "things are not real").

OGOING TRAUMATIC STRESS DISORDER

Criterion H: attribution
Disturbance is not due to medication, substance use, or other
illness. In addition to meeting criteria for diagnosis, an
individual experiences high levels of either of the following in
reaction to trauma-related stimuli:
1. Depersonalization: experience of being an outside observer of
or detached from oneself (e.g., feeling as if "this is not happening
to me" or one were in a dream).
2. Derealization: experience of unreality, distance, or distortion
(e.g., "things are not real").
References
American Psychiatric Association. (2013) Diagnostic and statistical
manual of mental disorders, (5th ed.). Washington, DC: Author.
(OTSD criteria adapted from DSM)
http://www.ptsd.va.gov/professional/pages/dsm5_criteria_ptsd.asp

Chapter 8: Treatment and Coping

If one accepts that there is such a diagnosis as OTSD then what is the treatment for it and how are people supposed to cope with it? When I was director of a counseling agency I learned that you never go to a Board of Directors meeting with a problem and not also possible solutions to present to the Board. So if I am going to suggest a diagnosis then it is incumbent upon me to suggest some treatment and coping skills.

Treatment and coping is a work in progress. Some of what helps me might not be for everyone else. I find the attitude of addiction treatment field has an "ongoing" focus and that works well when coping with OTSD. Treatment of OTSD borrows more from the Addictions field than from traditional mental health. Cognitive Behavioral Therapy uses a good bit of rational thinking. For example if a person has a fear that riding in an elevator will end up with the elevator crashing to the ground. A CBT therapist might ask them "What is the probability that will happen?" or "How many times has that actually happened to them?" and other questions that demonstrate the irrationality of their fear and the low probability of "X" event occurring. With OTSD the patient's fear that a traumatic event is going to happen is a rational reality experience-based fear. There is a good probability that bad outcomes will happen. It is insulting to the patient to suggest that everything is really safe and the fear that they experience is irrational.

TREATMENT

Treatment starts with the treatment provider being willing to accept OTSD and to accept the powerlessness of the treatment provider. Much of what the treatment provider is offering is traditional supportive psychotherapy. The attitude of the treatment provider includes the following:

–The goal of treatment is about management not about cure.
–The traditional social work task "instillation of hope" is one of your main tasks.
–Being well grounded in the 12 Steps is critical.
–Owning your own powerlessness is critical.
The OTSD person is not psychologically sick or mentally ill - OTSD is normal given the circumstances of ongoing trauma.

Resiliency????

A concept that is in the mental health literature that you read about frequently is "resiliency." There is a sort of odd message in this literature that suggest that if you have resiliency you will respond to trauma in the right way and not have any problems. One study offered the following definition of resiliency:
"Resiliency is defined by a lack of post traumatic stress disorder following trauma"
http://www.ncbi.nlm.nih.gov/pubmed/19593805
There is a subtle "blaming the victim" type of thinking that is inherent in the resiliency concept.

Victim blaming occurs when the victim(s) of a crime, or any wrongful act are held entirely or partially responsible for the transgressions committed against them (regardless of whether the victim actually had any responsibility for the incident)... William Ryan coined the phrase "blaming the victim" in his 1971 book Blaming the Victim. [3][4][5][6][7] In the book, Ryan described victim blaming as an ideology used to justify racism and social injustice against black people in the United States.[6] Ryan wrote the book to refute Daniel Patrick Moynihan's 1965 work The Negro Family: The Case for National Action (usually simply referred to as the Moynihan Report).
https://en.wikipedia.org/wiki/Victim_blaming
Below is a description from the Department of Veterans Affairs about PTSD origins. I emphasized the last sentence:

*PTSD is unique among psychiatric diagnoses because of the great importance placed upon the etiological agent, the traumatic stressor. In fact, one cannot make a PTSD diagnosis unless the patient has actually met the "stressor criterion," which means that he or she has been exposed to an historical event that is considered traumatic. Clinical experience with the PTSD diagnosis has shown, however, that there are individual differences regarding the capacity to cope with catastrophic stress. Therefore, while some people exposed to traumatic events do not develop PTSD, others go on to develop the full-blown syndrome. Such observations have prompted the recognition that trauma, like pain, is not an external phenomenon that can be completely objectified. Like pain, the traumatic experience is filtered through cognitive and emotional processes before it can be appraised as an extreme threat. Because of individual differences in this appraisal process, different people appear to have different trauma thresholds, some more protected from and some more vulnerable to developing clinical symptoms after exposure to extremely stressful situations. **Although there is currently a renewed interest in subjective aspects of traumatic exposure, it must be emphasized that events such as rape, torture, genocide, and severe war zone stress are experienced as traumatic events by nearly everyone.***

http://www.ptsd.va.gov/professional/pages/ptsd-overview.asp

I think that last sentence is critical for the treatment provider to acknowledge when dealing with persons with OTSD. OTSD persons are not persons who have a personal failure with not having developed enough "resiliency" to cope effectively with trauma. I suggest that in order to not "blame the victim" that the treatment provider avoid the concept of resiliency when treating OTSD.

COPING SKILLS

SKILL 1. Use the revised "Three C's" and revised 1st Step

In Al Anon they use the twelve steps and they have a slogan called "The three C's."

The "three C's" are:
-You did not cause the disease
-You can't cure the disease
-You can't control the disease

Now for Al Anon the "disease" is alcoholism. For OTSD the word "disease: is replaced with the word "trauma."

So the revised Three C's are:
-You did not cause the trauma
-You can't cure the trauma
-You can't control the trauma

It is important to note that with addictions treatment there is no "cure" of the addiction but there is management of how we respond to the addiction. Likewise there is no "cure" for OTSD. The only choices we have are how we manage our responses to trauma. Below are the 1st Step from Alcoholics Anonymous and then the revised 1st Step for OTSD:

"We admitted we were powerless over alcohol that our lives had become unmanageable."

Revised to:

"We admitted we were powerless over trauma that our lives had become unmanageable."

SKILL 2: Use the serenity Prayer as a guiding principal and sort of
"bloom where you are planted."

Al Anon literature notes that it is a spiritual program not a religious program. In 12 step programs the Serenity Prayer below is frequently recited:

God grant me the serenity
to accept the things I cannot change;
courage to change the things I can;
and wisdom to know the difference.

As I say that prayer nowadays I frequently stop after the first part. I admit to myself that the vast majority of things are things I cannot change. Of the small amount of things that are left on the list of things I can change- I don't always do such a good job at changing those things.
I do find that my new "life motto" helps with the things that I can change:

"If I am not in the hospital today and I feel well and I want to do something, I am going to do it now"

Some of the ways that I implement this life motto are:
-This has led me to take on projects at work, with my professional association, with my church and in my community. Sometimes this attitude keeps me too busy. I get out of balance.
-Physically I have lost so many options that I have shifted my focus into task that don't require physical activity that is beyond my capabilities. I research and write a good bit on various topics.
-I learned how to use video editing software to create webinars. I write Letters to the newspaper.
-I work on my blog and on a website for my professional association. My learning curve on computer skills has increased greatly. Not programing, just using the computer to help me with research, video editing, graphics and other "user" task. All of this is the "sort of bloom where you are planted" type of coping.

SKILL 3: Engage in your spirituality and community:

In 12 step programs they frequently talk about "a higher power" and several of the steps mention God. Below are the 12 steps of Alcoholics Anonymous.

1. We admitted we were powerless over alcohol - that our lives had become unmanageable.
2. Came to believe that a power greater than ourselves could restore us to sanity.
3. Made a decision to turn our will and our lives over to the care of God as we understood Him.
4. Made a searching and fearless moral inventory of ourselves.
5. Admitted to God, to ourselves, and to another human being the exact nature of our wrongs.
6. Were entirely ready to have God remove all these defects of character.
7. Humbly asked Him to remove our shortcomings.
8. Made a list of all persons we had harmed, and became willing to make amends to them all.
9. Made direct amends to such people wherever possible, except when to do so would injure them or others.
10. Continued to take personal inventory, and when we were wrong, promptly admitted it.
11. Sought through prayer and meditation to improve our conscious contact with God as we understood Him, praying only for knowledge of His will for us and the power to carry that out.
12. Having had a spiritual awakening as the result of these steps, we tried to carry this message to alcoholics, and to practice these principles in all our affairs.
http://www.aa.org/en_pdfs/smf-121_en.pdf

Below is my humble attempt to translate the AA 12 Steps into an OTSD 12 steps:

OTSD 12 STEPS

1. We admitted we were powerless over trauma - that our lives had become unmanageable.
2. Came to believe that a power greater than ourselves could restore us to have hope.
3. Made a decision to turn our will and our lives over to the care of God as we understood Him.
4. Made a searching and fearless inventory of our own limitations from living with OTSD.

5. Admitted to God, to ourselves, and to another human being the impact our trauma has had on our lives.

6. Were entirely ready to have God be a presence in our ongoing trauma.

7. Humbly asked Him to remove our urge to be in control.

8. Made a list of all persons God has put in our lives to help us cope with trauma.

9. Made direct acknowledgement and expressed appreciation to those persons.

10. Continued to monitor ourselves for trying to be in control of the uncontrollable and promptly admitted it.

11. Sought through prayer and meditation to improve our conscious contact with God as we understood Him, praying only for knowledge of His will for us and the power to carry that out.

12. Having had a spiritual awakening as the result of these steps, we tried to carry this message to other OTSD persons, and to practice these principles in all our affairs.

"While you pray, move your feet"

I have heard that an old Amish expression is "While you pray, move your feet." I have found that I am much more active with my church. I served on the Vestry, joined the building and grounds committee, go to the Men's breakfast bible study, volunteer when help is needed and take on the coffee hour preparations when it is near a holiday so I can bake lots of interesting items (I like to bake). Spirituality is both an "inside job" and being part of a community. For me to cope with OTSD I need to feel my own spiritual connection with God and I need to feel God's presence in others in my community.

When I was the sickest many people sent Get Well cards. I took all of those cards and I got a large poster board. I drew a huge heart on the poster board and then I attached all of the Get Well cards to the heart. For me it symbolized all of God's love coming through all of those people to me to help me cope. OTSD is not something you can manage all by yourself.

I greatly appreciated the Get Well cards. However there is a strange two edged sword component to receiving a Get Well card when you have OTSD. I can't "Get Well." The very nature of OTSD is that it is ongoing. My distorted thinking can hear "Get Well" as a command that I am unable to follow. So nowadays when a friend is sick and I have the urge to send a card, I pick a "thinking of you" type of card instead of a Get Well card.

SKILL 4: Identity and loss-Sublimation

Eric Erickson has eight stages and eight developmental tasks that are to be accomplished throughout life. During adolescence the task is "Identity vs. Role Confusion." So as an adult in my 50s my identity was fairly well established. OTSD with health consequences that involve loss of functioning challenges me daily to alter my identity and my concept of my self-of who I am as a person. http://en.wikipedia.org/wiki/Erik_Erikson

I used to play golf. I can't play golf anymore. I can't walk the golf course. I can't ever walk from where the cart path goes to my ball. I have fun memories of playing golf and I don't want to go out to the golf course and try to do some way of playing golf with my physical difficulties and then have that be my memory of playing golf.

I used to enjoy hiking in the Shenandoah National Park-up and down some mountains. There are many things that I used to enjoy doing. I have lost the ability to do those things and this impacts my sense of myself-my sense of identity.

Psychology has a concept called "sublimation.

Sublimation fuels positive productivity.

In chemistry, sublimation describes the conversion of a solid directly to a gas without passing through a liquid state (ie. think dry ice – ice evaporating without ever being water). In life, sublimation psychology can be thought of as your negative energy (solid) being transformed directly into a positive, productive behavior (gas) without experiencing the anger, anxiety and stress.

Sublimation is the mechanism by which we convert unproductive, mentally uncomfortable, emotional states into positive results. We are socially driven to find acceptable means through which we unleash the pent up energy created by situations

stimulating negative emotions. By sublimating, we convert the unproductive state into a productive behavior in order to stop the wheel of negativity from spinning.

http://www.drcoryalfers.com/sublimation-psychology/

I use a good bit of sublimation in my life now.

Chapter 9: Trish's experience

This section could not be written by me. It had to be written by Trish. And it is sort of awkward to decide where to put it in the body of the text. It was happening concurrently to my experience. It reminds me of reading about World War II when there could be actions in France and in North Africa and other places all at the same time but you can only read about them one at a time. So we decided to put Trish's experience here. I ask for your patience in putting the two experiences together.

Joe and I had been dating only three months when I learned life can take some dramatic turns when you least expect it. I drove to Harrisonburg one Friday evening in August, 2000 to meet Joe at his office. When I walked into the building I noticed a note on Joe's office door and then someone came into the waiting room and introduced himself to me. He was a friend of Joe's, David, and one of Joe's colleagues was with him. They told me Joe had been taken to the hospital earlier that day and David was going to take me over there to see him.

We got into the emergency department and Joe was in a cubicle on a stretcher. He looked gray and was very groggy. I thought maybe it was a heart problem, but he was admitted and the doctor said they had not determined the cause of a pain on his right side just below his ribs. They had given him a lot of pain medicine so he was not awake very much. At one point he woke up and asked me to go to his apartment and get his CPAP (Continuous Positive Air Pressure – for Sleep Apnea) machine and bring it to him. It was so strange to go into his home alone, like I was intruding. I got the machine and went back to the hospital. Joe woke up long enough to ask me to stay with him because he was afraid to be alone there. Of course I agreed to do that even though I had no idea what I was getting into.

I told the nurse I would be staying and she was very nice, brought me a blanket and a pillow. I settled into a recliner and tried to sleep, but that was impossible. I had wave after wave of panic sweep over me as I thought about what was happening and what might happen. I prayed for Joe and asked God to please not take him because he was needed by so many people in his life. I had met Joe's daughter and I knew they were very close. He had described his extended family and it was obvious they were a close-knit family. I thought of his patients and the impact of his work. Of course, I thought of myself, too. I had grown to love Joe in a short time and wanted to think we had a future to look forward to.

In between these thoughts and prayers Joe was visited by many people, coming to take blood or vital signs, medication and at one point they even brought in a portable machine to take an x-ray of his chest. I didn't think anything about that since I knew that was routine for a hospital admission. He woke up several times, sometimes wanting a cold compress on his forehead and sometimes just to ask about what was going on. The night went by quickly and not sleeping didn't seem to be very difficult. Joe encouraged me from time to time to go get something to eat and the nurses were so nice offering me coffee or milk and I discovered I still loved peanut butter on graham crackers which seem to be in good supply. All through that day various doctors came and talked to Joe, asking about his medical history and explaining some of the test results. They tried reducing the pain medication but soon discovered that the level of pain was still severe and so he was kept on it. Another evening of watching the sunset from the hospital room and then the dark.

It's never quiet or even very dark in the hospital at night, but there is strangeness about the night times there. I got as comfortable as I could and even though I had had no sleep the night before I was not tired and found it impossible to sleep. Again, a kind of panic would overcome me and I would start talking to God asking him for the courage to face whatever was ahead. I remembered all the things I had been learning in my new job as a hospice social worker, the kinds of things I would say to family members as they faced their fears. In between these thoughts and prayers I took care of Joe, cold compresses, answering his questions the best I could and wondered about tomorrow. Sometime during the night his pain subsided and the next day they talked about discharging him after a few more tests. I dashed to his house and took a shower and when I returned a different doctor was in the room talking to Joe.

He was telling Joe that the chest x-ray showed a mass on the left lobe of his lungs. He said he did not think this was the cause of Joe's pain, but it was certainly something that needed further attention. We were stunned since Joe had never smoked, never had an injury to his chest or any type of lung infection. He was discharged that evening and I went home with my son, Ben, who was seven at the time.

A few weeks later Joe had some more tests and then a meeting with a thoracic surgeon. He was very kind, but straightforward about the seriousness of Joe's situation. He even said Joe should be "getting his affairs in order" because he suspected the worse, small cell carcinoma of the lung. Joe and I could hardly say anything to each other as those words sunk into our awareness. I know we spent the rest of that day together, I had taken the rest of the day off from my job, but I do not remember anything until that evening when we picked up Ben from his afterschool program. We followed Joe to one of his favorite restaurants that was on the road he would take back home that night. We tried to eat, but that was not possible and we tried to tell Ben without showing our fear. That was not easy and all the way back to our apartment Ben asked questions and expressed the faith of a child that everything was going to be OK.

As the date of Joe's surgery approached it seemed I was getting all the lung CA cases at the hospice where I worked. It was a huge challenge to comfort and guide patients and their families through the process of their dying as I wondered about what I would be facing. I like challenges and somehow I was able to lose myself in my work each day, but nights after putting Ben to bed and talking to Joe by phone, I would toss and turn, hopeful, fearful, calm and terrified. Finally, the day of the surgery came and a lot of Joe's family members came including his son and daughter and their mother. I was meeting most of these people for the first time that day and there were some awkward moments. The surgery went a lot longer than anticipated, but finally the doctor came out and said with obvious relief to the hovering crowd, "it's not cancer, I don't know what it is, but it is not cancer!" It was such a relief to hear that, but I also felt some anxiety that the doctor truly did not know what it was. He said later that he just thought it was some kind of scar tissue and that was that. We all focused on Joe's recovery.

Joe asked me to stay with him at night in the hospital again. I was glad to do that and I could see it gave his family some comfort knowing I was there with him. The staff at UVA were not as welcoming as they had been at RMH and that certainly did not help what was already an uncomfortable situation. I sat in a hard chair, stayed cold all night, but also found comfort in being with Joe as he woke up frequently asking questions and needing things to be done for him. I have always had a good tolerance of the sight of blood and medical issues, but Joe's situation was difficult to watch. The incision was huge; he had chest tubes that allowed blood to drain and several IVs going. A lot of beeping sounds and any time he moved much or coughed (which he did a lot)blood would rush through the tube into a reservoir where it collected and was measured periodically. This was not a place for a faint hearted person and I was grateful I was able to handle it. Joe got discharged and after being so involved in his care for those few days it was hard to see him leave with his family and return to Harrisonburg where I would only see him on the weekends.

His mother moved in with him and I came on weekends as did some of his siblings and children. I remember taking Joe for slow walks around his street. He got stronger, returned to work and his mother went back to her home. Things were getting back to more of a routine. One night on the phone with Joe he mentioned having some odd symptoms and I remember telling him he should see the doctor. In the back of my mind I was still worried about his health and even the smallest problem scared me. After several trips to the doctor the symptoms got worse and finally someone recognized what was wrong and sent Joe by ambulance to UVA. I have to admit when I got that phone call I fell apart and was thinking it was something related to the lung mass and I just knew that could not be good. I left work picked up my son from school and went to the hospital where I met by Joe's mother and sister. The doctor came into the room and explained the diagnosis, Guillian-Barré syndrome. The myelin sheath on Joe's nerves was being destroyed by his own body. They explained the treatment, but also said his symptoms could get worse before the treatment was finished and recovery would be slow.

Joe got discharged on Christmas Eve, a hectic time. I had taken my son to his grandmother's house, wrapped his presents then left to get back to Charlottesville for Joe.

At the hospital, just before leaving I noticed one side of his face was drooping! He had been moved to a different floor earlier and so when I told the nurses my observation their response floored me. They said they thought he always looked that way! An emergency consult was placed with neurology and after the exam they concluded it was just the progression of the Guillian-Barré syndrome and not a stroke so he was finally discharged. Christmas Eve, we get prescriptions filled, get a walker and shower chair to use at my apartment. Joe could not go back to his townhouse because of the stairs so he was going to stay with me for a few days or until he could lift his legs high enough to climb stairs. Joe made one request that night that I take him to a midnight mass at the local Catholic Church. We went early knowing it would take Joe a while to walk into the church and he wanted to be sure and sit near a door so we could get back out easily. I felt like I was with a different person. Joe was moving like an elderly person, his mood and affect somber, sad.

He was very tired when we returned to my apartment. Because the syndrome had progressed to the nerves in his face Joe was unable to close his eyes. The doctor had told me to put moist compresses on his eyes and then tape them shut so he could sleep. Joe also uses a CPAP and so with that and the eyes taped he looked pretty bad. Sometime during the night he woke up in a panic when he tried to open his eyes, did not remember the tape and so thought he had gone blind! He started tearing off the bandages and his CPAP and was almost hysterical as I tried to tell him what was wrong. He got settled again and we slept for a few hours. The next day we went to Richmond so I could be with my family for Christmas. Joe had difficulty with his eyes staying full of tears since he could not blink and the paralysis had made it difficult for him to chew. Later, he talked about how uncomfortable he felt about the way he looked and having to use a walker.

A few days later he was able to lift his legs enough to get up stairs and so he wanted to go home. So the day before New Year's Eve I took him to Harrisonburg and his mother returned from Baltimore to help through this recovery. On New Year's Eve I got an idea and Joe's mother and Emily thought it sounded great. So we got busy calling as many of Joe's friends as we could and put together plans for a surprise party at his office. Most folks were planning to go to the First Night celebration that night and so stopping by the office for some refreshments with Joe would be a bonus. We got everything together and set up at his office and people started arriving and kept coming in all evening. At one point a group of singers came and sang for Joe. He was so moved by all the love and good wishes he received that night, it really boosted him up.

Our lives became a little more routine after that. I went back to Charlottesville, my son and my job with hospice. Joe was involved in physical therapy several times a week. On weekends I would visit him and I could see incredible progress. He went back to work and his mother returned to her home. By spring we were looking forward to Emily's graduation from high school and Joe was back out of the golf course. All the fear and distress subsided and we all seemed to recover from the trauma of that winter.

Late that summer I lost a dear old friend. I stayed with him the last few days and watched him fade away. I had done this many times with my hospice patients but it was a very different experience for me when it was someone I had known and loved for a long time. I found myself thinking about Joe and how afraid I was to lose him. After my friend died there were moments when I thought how wonderful it would be just to see his smile again or hear his voice. The finality of death is so harsh. I wanted the world to just stop for a while so I could adjust to this change. I kept thinking I needed more time to think and feel. The whole experience left me with a greater appreciation for the mysteries of time, life and death and most of all, love. So when Joe asked me to marry him and start a life together in Harrisonburg I had no hesitation. I left my job and Ben and I moved into a house in Harrisonburg two months before the wedding. We worked hard to plan a happy celebration of our love for each other and our families. Our children all took part in the ceremony and I felt a great deal of peace and hope for our future. Joe and I had a honeymoon in Ireland where I met a lot more of his family and we spent hours walking and touring around the country.

We had almost three good years and then in the spring of 2005 Joe got a cold that would not go away. It got worse and so he went to the doctor. He was treated for bronchitis, but the x-ray showed something more and so we were sent back to Charlottesville. After several tests we were told it looked like Joe had cancer. Another mass was in the left lobe of his lung and so surgery was planned right away. I felt anxiety about this, but something else inside me was calm and determined. We had been through this before and it turned out OK, I knew Joe was strong and he would put up a fight. After three hours in surgery the doctor came out and told us the mass had calcified and getting it out was tedious and slow. The good news was they were sure it was not cancer. Three more hours and they were done, but the doctor said he had concerns about Joe's voice. Some nerves had been cut during surgery, one to the vocal chords and one that inflated the lung. They took me to Joe in the recovery area and told me to try to get him to speak. I don't remember what I said or asked him, but he did wake up and speak to me. Everyone was very happy about that. He was in ICU for the first night, but after that I stayed with him until he came home. His recovery went well, but once in a while I felt some intense anxiety and wondered about complications like the ones in 2000-2001. I tried to think positive and was able to do that most of the time. But then he would have a coughing spell or complain of an ache or pain or even just fatigue and I would slip into that scary place. I noticed my son paid close attention and would get anxious if Joe had any physical problems. When I saw that I was quick to pull myself together and assure Ben that everything was fine. That made me feel better, too.

Late in 2006, Joe and I had spent the weekend at a craft fair. Late afternoon of the second day he said he was feeling sick with nausea. We packed up and went home. Joe started throwing up violently as soon as we got in the house. This went on for a little while and I decided it was time to take him to the hospital, I felt fear and a sense of urgency. At the hospital they started running tests and we were there for several hours and Joe got worse. He started running a high fever and was congested. He had aspirated and gotten pneumonia! He was admitted and I stayed with him. A friend agreed to take Ben home and get him to school the next morning. I stayed at the hospital the next day and then Joe insisted I go home that night. That night I got sick and started throwing up. I guess I caught whatever Joe had. It was terrible, and lasted several days. Ben got it, too. During that time I tried to keep up with Joe's condition and that got to be terrible as well. He had developed an ileus and so they were doing x-rays almost daily of his abdomen. He told me the doctors had found an aneurysm and they wanted him to get a follow up at UVA which they arranged. By Friday he was discharged and I was able to get him home. I had recovered from the stomach bug, but I did not feel well.

Joe had the tests at UVA and they found three aneurysms and said he needed surgery to fix them. I started to feel some panic at times as I wondered what lay ahead. The surgery took a longer time because they found more aneurysms. The surgeon said they had to cut through the nervous system that controls the movement of food through the digestive tract. He said this would take time to heal, but most people recover completely. I thought to myself, you don't know Joe, he is not like most people. I stayed with him and each day I could see him getting weaker as he struggled to eat or drink anything. By the time he was discharged I had to run to the nearest store to buy him some sweatpants because the pants he wore into the hospital a week earlier just fell off him even with his belt in the last notch. The doctor assured me he would get better, it would just take time.

We were only home a few days when I knew something was wrong and took Joe to our family doctor. He said he was dehydrated and needed IV fluids which could be done at our local hospital. That helped for a few days and then the nausea, vomiting and diarrhea got even worse and so we ended up back at UVA. This happened many times and Joe continued to lose weight and strength. I kept asking about what could be done to improve his digestion and I kept being told to just try offering him small amounts of different things until I found what he could tolerate. I tried everything! Nothing worked and I kept taking him back to the doctors and they kept sending me home and telling me to try harder! The doctors said they wanted to do the second surgery even though I protested because of Joe's decline. Things got even worse after the second surgery and there were multiple admissions to RMH and UVA. Joe got down to 165 lbs., a hundred pounds less than when he had the first surgery. He slept most of the time and lost all interest in food saying he felt no hunger and asked me to just let him sleep. He even got angry with me at times and that hurt so much.

I felt so alone and lost in the huge industry of medicine, I was just one person and no one was listening to me. I told the doctors finally that I could see Joe was dying, wasting away and that I could not take him home, but would not leave him in the care of the surgeon. The surgeon insisted the surgery was a success, he could not see his patient was dying. I said rather loudly that I was not leaving the hospital until a gastroenterologist and a dietician were consulted. I heard the doctor get on the phone and ask for "backup" so I realized he finally heard me. Within two hours of getting to the hospital that day Joe was admitted and an N/G tube put in so he could receive liquid supplements directly into his stomach, bypassing the area that had all the nerve damage. He started getting better and I took him home. It took several more months to get him built up again. I went back to work in October and he continued to recover at home.

I lost another older friend in November. I stayed with her the last few nights she was on earth and followed her wishes for her last days and her burial. Again, I was so shocked by the abrupt end to life. The process of dying can be slow and even peaceful, but death seems so sudden, a last breath and then nothing, no more. I started to feel numb after that and just focused on whatever task I had in front of me. I also started noticing a strange tightness in my jaw, especially in the morning. I started waking up a lot at night with pain in my neck, jaw, shoulders. I realized I was all "squeezed up" like I was anticipating a blow to my head and upper body, like a boxer in the ring with his gloved hands up in front of his face, shoulders pulled up almost to his ears. It got worse and my jaw became very painful, it was hard to chew food. I finally went to the dentist, got physical therapy, a mouth guard to wear at night and more physical therapy. This was not going away very easily. I was struggling, putting up a fight against some imaginary foe.

Joe kept having regular check- ups at UVA and in the fall of 2009 another aneurysm was found that required surgery. A couple hours into the procedure the surgeon came out and said there were problems. The scar tissue was so dense and bled so much they could not continue and so they would have to "close him up and find another way." The doctor said he would never do surgery on Joe through the abdomen again, it was too risky. Any future aneurysms would have to be repaired other ways whenever that was possible. They kept Joe a few days and then said they would send him home for a few days and bring him back for a different surgical procedure. I was not comfortable with the idea of taking him home for a day or two and then back to the hospital, I thought the drives back and forth would be too much for him and told the doctors that. They agreed to keep him and do the procedure, but then explained he would have to wait a few weeks for the second part of the procedure. I had started a new job and so I explained what was going on and arranged to have time off so I could be with Joe at critical times. In the back of my mind I wondered what would happen if there were complications like before. Would a new employer be understanding and supportive? We were finally recovering from the financial strain on 2007 and I was fully aware of how much I needed to keep this new job.

Joe had a few minor problems with the procedures, but he did recover quickly. I got settled into the new job and things went smoothly for about a year. Then a check-up found another new aneurysm behind his right knee. Another surgery was scheduled that was supposed to involve a few days at UVA. We were there for a week, but again, his recovery went OK. They don't tell you much about the possible complications from popliteal aneurysm surgery. Joe has more nerve damage; his right leg bothers him a lot. We're not sure why, but he has lots of pain when he walks. The doctors don't have an explanation. He can't do a lot of things he used to enjoy. He no longer plays golf, long walks and hiking are impossible and then this summer I realized he was struggling to mow the grass. I have gotten one of our son's friends to come every week to mow and Joe really does appreciate that. It's hard for him to ask for help, I have to pay closer attention and offer it.

This has been a journey for both of us. Along with the tension and anxiety I developed some emotional numbness and at times became aware of some bitterness in my soul. I have had periods of experiencing a hyper-startle response to sudden noises or movement. And I have found this whole experience very difficult to talk about because it can bring up intense emotions and a sense of vulnerability that I struggle to accept. I have also found that I can get angry so easily when I have to deal with the systems that make health care in our country so difficult to manage. In 2012 I started doing some things to take better care of myself because I did not like how I had started to feel most of the time. I took training in Transcendental Meditation and practice daily now. I also started taking riding lessons and have continued to "horse around" with friends at a stable about 30 minutes from my home. The work with horses has expanded to include equine assisted therapy (EAGALA) which is now offered to veterans in our area. I am taking training toward certification in this therapeutic model and volunteer weekly at that stable to share the healing power of horses with others. I also find it very helpful to take walks several times a week. And I pray, a lot. At bedtime I go through a ritual of reflecting on the positive experiences from my day, what I appreciate and the gratitude I feel. This has helped me look for and recognize those things more easily. I have difficulty with religion sometimes, but I know I have become a more spiritual person, thanking God every day for everything. I sometimes falter, but I am going to keep practicing these things, it is the only way I will get better.

EPILOGUE

I have had over 20 hospital admissions, several surgeries and several procedures in the hospital. I now have 18 consecutive months without a hospitalization. I view it as a gift from God

While writing this paper I had my annual MRI at UVA to check on my aneurysms. The surgeon called to tell me that the native artery on the right popliteal artery had enlarged from 31mm to 44mm and surgery was necessary to tie off the blood vessels and prevent the aneurysm from rupturing. This was the artery that had the bypass graph repair.

Once again I learn that not being in the hospital today does not mean anything about tomorrow. I continue to cope each day and I know I only have *"One Day At A Time"* to live, and no guarantee of tomorrow. For me each morning I still say my motto: